Searchlight
BOOKS™

Animal
Superpowers

Dancing Bees

and Other Amazing Communicators

Mary Lindeen

Lerner Publications ◆ Minneapolis

Lerner Publications Company
A division of Lerner Publishing Group, Inc.
241 First Avenue North
Minneapolis, MN 55401 USA

For reading levels and more information, look up this title
at www.lernerbooks.com.

Library of Congress Cataloging-in-Publication Data

Names: Lindeen, Mary, author.
Title: Dancing bees and other amazing communicators / by Mary Lindeen.
Description: Minneapolis : Lerner Publications, [2017] | Series: Searchlight books.
    Animal superpowers | Audience: Ages 8–11. | Audience: Grades 4 to 6. | Includes
    bibliographical references and index.
Identifiers: LCCN 2016014197 (print) | LCCN 2016025632 (ebook) | ISBN 9781512425451
    (lb : alk. paper) | ISBN 9781512431148 (pb : alk. paper) | ISBN 9781512428216 (eb pdf)
Subjects: LCSH: Animal communication—Juvenile literature. | Animal behavior—Juvenile
    literature.
Classification: LCC QL751.5 .L547 2017 (print) | LCC QL751.5 (ebook) |
    DDC 591.59—dc23

LC record available at https://lccn.loc.gov/2016014197

Manufactured in the United States of America
2-45436-23257-2/20/2018

Contents

Chapter 1

HUMMING GIRAFFES

Communicating with one another helps animals survive. It also makes them fascinating to study. For instance, scientists were surprised to learn that giraffes hum! Researchers recorded giraffes at night in three zoos. These recordings revealed that the giraffes were humming. This surprised the scientists and zookeepers, who usually aren't in the giraffe barn at night.

Giraffes are fairly quiet animals. What types of sounds do they make?

Coughing, Hissing, and Growling

Giraffes make only a few sounds. They are more vocal during mating season. Males make a coughing sound to attract females. The coughing lets females know the males are near.

Giraffes also make hissing and growling sounds. A mother giraffe might hiss or make a low growl to keep her baby close to her. Giraffes also hiss or growl to warn other giraffes of danger.

Giraffes also communicate by rubbing their necks and leaning against one another. This is known as necking.

A Pain in the Neck

For a long time, scientists believed giraffes were quiet because of their necks. Researchers thought a giraffe's long neck probably made it hard for the animal to make most vocal sounds. An adult giraffe's neck is about 6 feet (1.8 meters) long. Air has to travel a long way to get from a giraffe's lungs to its mouth. It takes a lot of effort to push air that far.

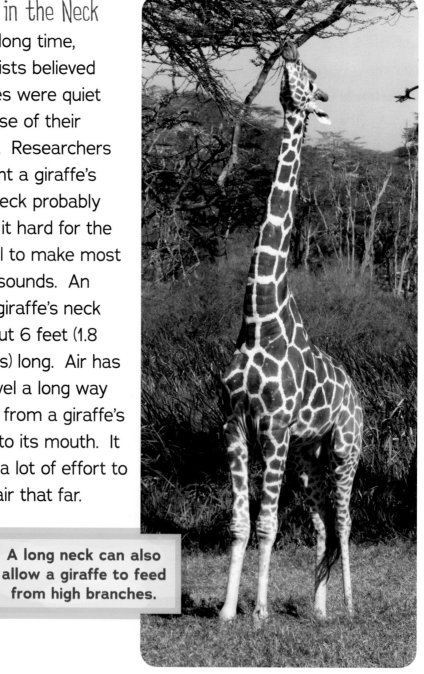

A long neck can also allow a giraffe to feed from high branches.

High and Low

But scientists knew giraffes live in organized social groups. Other social animals, such as elephants, communicate within their groups all the time. So researchers wondered how giraffes were communicating if they weren't making many sounds.

They thought giraffes might use sounds that were too low-pitched for humans to hear. They also thought giraffes might rely on visual signals. Giraffes have good eyesight. Their eyesight and their long necks make it possible for them to see one another over trees and when they're far apart.

These giraffes can easily see one another while they feed.

Compare It!

Researchers also used recordings to learn about another incredible animal communicator. They could see that hole-in-the-head frogs were inflating the pouches on their throats, but no one could hear any sounds. The scientists studied their recordings and realized these frogs send and receive sounds that are too high-pitched for humans to hear. Scientists think these sounds allow the frogs to communicate above the noise of the waterfalls and rushing rivers in their habitat. Hole-in-the-head frogs are the only species of frog known to communicate this way.

Hole-in-the-head frogs live in the tropical rain forests of Borneo.

Humming could be one way a giraffe keeps in contact with other giraffes in the darkness.

Marco! Polo!

Scientists still don't know why giraffes hum. They might be communicating. Or humming might just be a sound giraffes make when they're sleeping, like snoring. One theory is that giraffes hum to let others in their herd know where they are. This would be a useful way to keep everyone in the group together at night. More research will be needed to find out why giraffes hum.

Chapter 2

DANCING BEES

A honeybee flies out of the hive in search of food. She's in luck! She finds a flower bed full of spring blossoms. This honeybee is a scout. Her job is to look for sources of food. She collects as much nectar as she can from the flowers in the flower bed. Then she returns to the hive. She shares the nectar she's collected with the other bees. And then she dances.

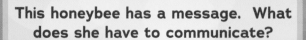

This honeybee has a message. What does she have to communicate?

Dancing is an important form of communication for honeybees. It allows one bee to share information with hundreds of other bees at the same time. A hive might have as many as eighty thousand bees in it. Sharing information quickly and efficiently is important so other bees will know where honey can be found or when help is needed.

These honeybees return to their hive with nectar for honey and food for the bee colony and queen bee.

These bees share information by doing the waggle dance.

The Waggle Dance

The scout goes to a place in the hive that's like a dance floor for bees. She runs in a figure-eight pattern, wagging her body from side to side. This special pattern of running and wagging is called the waggle dance. It tells other bees where to find more of the food that the scout has just brought. A shorter dance means the food is close. A longer dance means the food is farther away. The direction of the dance also tells the other bees which direction to fly to find the food.

Shake and Tremble

Honeybees do other kinds of dances too. If a particularly rich source of food has been found, a worker bee might shake her body as she moves through the hive. This shake dance tells bees that don't usually collect food to watch the waggle dance and help collect nectar too. A worker bee does a tremble dance when more bees in the hive are needed to help turn nectar into honey. She shakes her legs to make her body shiver.

Dancing can tell other bees to get busy and help make more honey.

Compare It!

An albatross is a bird that lives near the ocean. Like the honeybee, an albatross communicates by dancing. Two or more birds will bow, sway, shake their heads, and clap their bills open and shut in a mating dance. The birds might also lift their wings, point their beaks to the sky, and call out. Once a male and a female become partners, the two birds will stay together for the rest of their lives.

Albatrosses have the largest wingspan of any animal in nature.

Bee-lieve It!

Honeybees also use the waggle dance to tell other bees where to find water if the hive is getting too hot. They use the waggle dance to tell other bees where to find a new home if the hive is getting too small. Scientists think bees can communicate more than forty million different messages using the waggle dance. Humans are the only animals that share more messages with one another. Honeybees are small, but they are big communicators.

Good communication is good for a beehive.

Chapter 3

CLICKING DOLPHINS

A baby dolphin gets separated from its mother. The baby makes a clicking sound. The mother also makes a clicking sound. Soon the baby and its mother are back together again. They used echolocation to find each other in the water.

Dolphins use clicking to communicate. How do they create the clicking?

Dolphins use echolocation by making sound waves and sending them out through the water. The sound waves are produced in a dolphin's nasal passages, just below the dolphin's blowhole and right behind the melon on its forehead. Dolphins send sound waves out ahead of them as they move through the water. Then they measure the amount of time it takes for those waves to bounce back to them. This helps dolphins find food, other dolphins, and dangerous animals or objects in the water.

The melon is the lump on a dolphin's forehead.

Compare It!

Deathwatch beetles also communicate by making clicking sounds. These beetles use their heads to make these sounds, just as dolphins do. But the beetles use the outside of their heads to communicate, not the inside.

Deathwatch beetles make tunnels in wood. A deathwatch beetle looking for a mate will hit its head against the sides of its tunnel, making a clicking sound. Another beetle can follow this sound to find a mate.

Long ago, people who were awake at night to watch over sick loved ones often heard beetles clicking. The sound became associated with keeping a deathwatch.

Pod Power

Dolphins are very social animals. They live in groups called pods. They have to communicate with one another to keep the pod together. Staying together helps keep them safe from predators. It also helps them hunt for food. The pod works together to gather groups of fish. Then the dolphins take turns swimming in the middle of the fish, where it's easier to catch and eat the food.

These dolphins work together to catch sardines.

Squeals and Whistles

Dolphins are almost always making some kind of sound. The water they swim in isn't always clear. They cannot count on being able to see one another. So they use clicking sound waves. They also use their voices to make squealing and whistling sounds. Different vocal sounds have different meanings. Sometimes dolphins sound as if they're having conversations when they're vocalizing. That's because dolphins are the only animals other than humans to take turns when they communicate.

Dolphins rely on sound for most of their communication.

SOME DOLPHINS CAN DO FLIPS OR
SPINS THROUGH THE AIR!

Flippers and Tails

Using touch and body language is another way dolphins communicate. They slap their tails and flippers as a warning or to play. They also bump one another. Soft bumps show friendship. Hard bumps show anger. They jump and leap out of the water too. This helps them watch out for enemies. It is also a way of having fun. Dolphins use their impressive powers of communication for work and play.

Chapter 4

RUMBLING ELEPHANTS

An elephant herd heads to a watering hole. The herd leader keeps the group together by making very low sounds as she walks. She is rumbling. If one of the other elephants falls behind and loses sight of the group, it will still get to the watering hole. It can listen to the rumbling and know just where to go to find the herd.

Elephants can do more than rumble. How many sounds can elephants make?

Elephants are remarkable communicators. They use all of their senses for communication. They use sound most of all. Elephants can make more than seventy different kinds of vocal sounds. They can make loud roars. They can make gentle grunts. They can make all kinds of noises, including snorts, barks, groans, and growls. Humans can hear all of these elephant sounds. What humans cannot hear are the low rumbles that elephants send to one another.

Different types of elephant sounds can send different messages.

Compare It!

Like elephants, prairie dogs use a variety of vocal sounds to communicate. Some scientists think prairie dogs have a more complex vocal language than any other animal except humans. A prairie dog bark is often a warning that an enemy is near. It also tells other prairie dogs what kind of enemy is near and what the enemy looks like! Prairie dogs are such amazing communicators that they can create new calls to describe something they've never seen before.

Prairie dogs are social rodents that live in colonies in underground tunnels.

Built for Sound

The size and structure of an elephant's head, along with its huge body, make it easy for the elephant to make rumbling sounds. Think about how a tuba can make lower sounds than a trumpet. In the same way, an elephant's size and bone structure allow it to make very low sounds. Elephant bodies can detect these low sounds. They have big ears. They also have sensitive pads on the bottoms of their feet. Rumbles travel through the air and the ground. Scientists believe elephants can both hear and feel the rumbling messages being sent by other elephants.

Elephants may be many different sizes, but they all communicate by rumbling.

Communication Nation

Elephants can live a long time. They have large brains and live in social groups. Their survival depends on being able to communicate in meaningful ways.

Low sounds travel farther than high sounds. So rumbling allows elephants to communicate over long distances. This helps the animals find mates. Adult males and females live in separate groups. Sending rumbles over a long distance is one way for males and females to find each other for mating.

Elephants communicate in social groups.

Adult elephants need to communicate with one another to keep their young safe.

Elephants also work together to protect their young. Adult elephants do not have many natural predators. But baby elephants can be attacked by lions and other animals. A mother elephant can send an alarm signal if her baby is in danger. Other elephants will run to help. Elephants can also travel a long way to find members of their families. Researchers have wondered how elephants know when and where to find one another. Rumbling is one possible explanation.

From Head to Tail

An elephant's trunk is an important part of its communication system. Elephants use their trunks for breathing. They also use their trunks for smelling and touching. Elephants can smell the ground to find out if a herd member or an enemy is nearby. A mother elephant uses her trunk to send gentle nudges to her calf. Elephants gently wrap their trunks together, much like humans hug or hold hands. An elephant even uses its trunk to slap an enemy.

These young elephants are playing together.

Elephants will slap trunks or butt heads to fight.

Other parts of an elephant's body can send messages too. When an elephant wants to scare an enemy, it spreads out its ears and lifts its head to make itself look bigger. Elephants use their heads and bodies to gently bump one another in play. They can also ram one another in aggression. An elephant with its chin up and its tail in the air sends the message that it's scared or excited. Elephants have a lot to say, and they have lots of ways to say it.

Chapter 5

BOBBING BIRDS-OF-PARADISE

A male bird-of-paradise turns around and around. He bobs up and down. He flaps his wings. He opens and closes a beautiful crest of feathers on his head. He swishes his body back and forth. He swings his long tail feathers. He's looking good. He's also looking for a mate. He knows that showing off his fancy feathers is the best way to find a female.

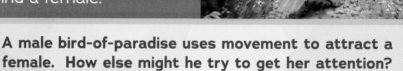

A male bird-of-paradise uses movement to attract a female. How else might he try to get her attention?

The main goal of a male bird-of-paradise is to attract females for mating. He does everything he can to persuade a female bird that he is the best choice for her. He might begin by making a series of loud calls. This lets any females in the area know where he is. Bird-of-paradise calls are as varied as the birds' feathers. Some calls sound like notes in a song. Some sound like humming or clicking. Others sound like hissing.

There are almost forty different species of birds-of-paradise.

This male bird-of-paradise displays his bright feathers to catch a female's attention.

Fine-Feathered Friends

Once a male gets a female's attention, he uses his feathers and body posture to keep it. The males have especially fancy feathers in many bright colors and patterns. Some birds even have patches of brightly colored bare skin. These bright, beautiful colors help attract a female.

Birds-of-paradise live in the tropical forests of Southeast Asia.

Some males have very unusual feathers. Those with long feathers shake these dramatic whips and streamers for maximum effect. Other males fluff and fan bunches of feathers on their heads, bodies, or tails to make themselves look more striking. This fluttering and fanning helps a male bird tell a female that he would be a good mate.

Female birds-of-paradise feathers help them blend in with the trees while the birds tend to their eggs and babies.

Shall We Dance?

Male birds-of-paradise also do different kinds of dances to attract females. Some dances happen high in the trees. The male turns around in circles or bounces on a branch or vine. Some males hang upside down to get noticed. Other birds clear an area on the forest floor to dance. Sometimes several males dance in the same spot. The dances might last for hours. The females watching the dances use their own body postures to show that they've chosen their partners.

Compare It!

Caribbean reef squid are greenish-brown sea creatures that can change color. They may turn pale to hide from a predator or reddish brown to blend into a coral reef. They can also create patterns of spots, stripes, and bands of color on their skin. A reef squid can even display two different patterns at the same time. A male can have one color pattern on its right side to send a message to an enemy and another color pattern on its left side to send a different message to a mate. That's some colorful communication!

The different colors on either side of this Caribbean reef squid communicate different messages at the same time.

Now You're Talking

The many species of birds-of-paradise are each unique in their own way, yet they have a lot in common. Other animal communicators are a lot like that too. They have many interesting differences but also many ways in which they are the same. Studying animal communication can help us learn more about animals. We can find out what animals need by learning to read the messages they send.

We can learn a lot about animals from the many ways they communicate.

Extinct Animal Superpowers

- Hadrosaurs were dinosaurs that had large crests on their heads. A hadrosaur could make a low call by forcing air though the hollow spaces in its crest. The call probably sounded a lot like a tuba.

- Millions of passenger pigeons used to fly in flocks that were hundreds of miles long. It took a lot of communication within a flock to keep this many birds together. They communicated using wing flaps, coos, and other cries.

- Steller's sea cows belonged to the same family as manatees and lived in the ocean. The sea cows had two short, thick arms that they used for moving around and communicating with other sea cows. Sometimes they used their arms for fighting or even embracing others.

Glossary

call: the cry of an animal

crest: a tuft of feathers or a growth on top of an animal's head

echolocation: the process of finding objects by using sound waves

mate: the male or female partner of a pair of animals

mating: joining together for breeding

pattern: a repeating arrangement of colors, shapes, and figures

predator: an animal that hunts other animals for food

social: together in a friendly and helpful way

species: one of the groups into which plants and animals are sorted according to their common features

vocal: having to do with the voice

Learn More about Animal Communicators

Books

Davies, Nicola. *Talk, Talk, Squawk! A Human's Guide to Animal Communication*. Somerville, MA: Candlewick, 2011. This book unlocks the mysteries of how animals talk and squawk to one another.

Hirsch, Rebecca E. *Humpback Whales: Musical Migrating Mammals*. Minneapolis: Lerner Publications, 2015. Discover how a humpback whale uses "music" to communicate with other whales.

Kalman, Bobbie. *How and Why Do Animals Communicate?* New York: Crabtree, 2015. This book shows how animals communicate to share information, attract mates, or scare away enemies.

Websites

The Kids' Science Challenge: Animal Smarts
http://www.kidsciencechallenge.com/year-four/as.php
Learn how animal communication is connected to animal intelligence.

PBS Kids: Prairie Dog Calls
http://pbskids.org/dragonflytv/show/prairiedogcalls.html
Watch a video showing how prairie dogs communicate by barking and how researchers collect data to learn more about these animals.

Wonderopolis: How Do Animals Communicate?
http://wonderopolis.org/wonder/how-do-animals-communicate
Check out this website to read or listen to an article about animal communication and watch a short video about dolphin communication.

Index

Photo Acknowledgments

The images in this book are used with the permission of: © Martin Schutt/AFP/Getty Images, p. 4; © Manoj Shah/Getty Images, p. 5; © blickwinkel/Alamy, pp. 6, 25, 33; © Attila Jandi/Shutterstock.com, p. 7; © Sam Hue/Alamy, p. 8; © LOOK Die Bildagentur der Fotografen/Alamy, p. 9; © sumikophoto/Shutterstock.com, p. 10; © zlikovec/Shutterstock.com, p. 11; © Scott Camazine/Alamy, p. 12; © Kim Taylor/naturepl.com, p. 13; © Kent Kobersteen/Getty Images, p. 14; © Scott Camazine/Getty Images, p. 15; © Cultura RM/Alamy, p. 16; © Gervasio S. _ Eureka_89/Shutterstock.com, p. 17; © FLPA/Alamy, p. 18; © Steve Bloom Images/Alamy, p. 19; © Ton Koene/VWPics/Alamy, p. 20; © Karen Debler/Alamy, p. 21; © v.shlichting/Shutterstock.com, p. 22; © Bill Gozansky/Alamy, p. 23; © Max Allen/Alamy, p. 24; © Eyal Bartov/Alamy, p. 26; © robertharding/Alamy, p. 27; © Juniors Bildarchiv GmbH / Alamy, p. 28; © Photoshot License Ltd / Alamy, p. 29; © Tim Laman/Getty Images, pp. 30, 31; © Herianus Herianus/Alamy, pp. 32, 36; © National Geographic Creative/Alamy, p. 34; © Mark Conlin/Alamy, p. 35; © Florilegius/Alamy, p. 37.

Front cover: © l i g h t p o e t /Shutterstock.com.

Main body text set in Adrianna Regular 14/20.
Typeface provided by Chank.